This is the true story of Jimmy,
a baby koala joey.

Jimmy the Joey

The True Story of an Amazing Koala Rescue

by **Deborah Lee Rose** and **Susan Kelly**
Photographs by Susan Kelly

NATIONAL GEOGRAPHIC

WASHINGTON, D.C.

Tiny and smooth as a pink jelly bean, a new baby koala crawled into his mother's warm pouch.

Baby koalas are called joeys. The little joey grew and grew, until he could pop his furry head up and wriggle his whole body out of the pouch.

The joey and his mother lived in Australia, like all wild koalas. His mother needed lots to eat, to give her energy and help her make milk for her baby. She got her food and water from the leaves of the tall eucalyptus trees in the forest.

Many trees in the forest had been cut down to make room for roads and people's houses. The mother koala needed to find a new tree with plenty of fresh leaves to eat. One starry night, with her joey holding tight to her fur, the mother koala climbed slowly down to the ground. She headed for a patch of trees across a big road. Suddenly, the joey saw bright lights from a car. His body hit the ground hard. He squeaked and squealed for his mother, but she didn't answer.

The next morning, a workman found the little koala lying by the road. The koala ambulance came and took the joey to the Koala Hospital.

To keep him warm, hospital volunteers wrapped the joey in a soft wool pouch. They called him Jimmy. He was just six months old, and very small.

Jimmy looked like a teddy bear with fluffy ears, but he wasn't a bear. Like kangaroos, koalas are marsupials—mammals that grow up in their mothers' pouches.

Cheyne, the hospital's wildlife biologist, listened to Jimmy's heart with her stethoscope. It was beating fast, just like a little boy's or girl's heart.

Jimmy was too young to go back to the forest alone. A specially trained volunteer named Barb took him home with her. She didn't smell or feel like his mother, but in her arms Jimmy felt safe and cozy. He nuzzled his head against her chest, and fell fast asleep.

Jimmy slept in a laundry basket filled with soft blankets. When he woke, he was always hungry and slurped down the baby koala formula Barb gave him.

"That's my boy," said Barb, just as if he were her very own baby. Barb brought Jimmy to the Koala Hospital each week for his checkup. First, he touched noses with everyone to say "hello." Then, Cheyne weighed and measured him to see how fast he was growing.

Week by week, Jimmy grew bigger and stronger, until he could race across the slippery hospital floor. Sometimes he hitched a ride, grabbing tight to Cheyne's leg. "That tickles!" Cheyne laughed, when his little claws dug in.

Jimmy was curious about everything, and he climbed up everywhere he could—even to the top of people's heads!

O ne day Barb put a branch full of leaves in Jimmy's basket. He knew that smell! Jimmy took a deep sniff of each leaf. He started munching . . .

. . . and munching.

Eating eucalyptus leaves made Jimmy smell like mint candy!

By his first birthday, Jimmy was big enough to move to the hospital's tree yard with the other koalas. He had never seen another koala before, except his mother. In the hospital trees he met Twinkles, a girl joey who loved to climb. Jimmy wanted to learn to climb, too!

Barb lifted him onto one of the tree trunks.

Getting up a real tree was hard at first. Jimmy dug his sharp claws into the rough bark and pushed with his strong legs.

He was climbing! Higher and higher Jimmy went, leaping from branch to branch, trying to reach Twinkles perched high above him.

From that day on, Jimmy lived outside with the other koalas.

Months went by. High in the branches, Jimmy started to make loud, bellowing sounds like snoring. These were grown-up koala sounds! None of the hospital volunteers fed Jimmy formula anymore, or hugged him. Now he had to get all his food from the trees himself and learn to live wild again. Finally, Jimmy was ready.

Cheyne put a tag on his ear to show he had been at the Koala Hospital, in case he ever needed help. Barb drove him to a protected forest area.

She carried his basket to the base of a thick, tall tree. As soon as she let him out, Jimmy ran right up the trunk. "Go, Jim!" called Barb proudly, as she watched him climb. She knew she was really saying goodbye.

When he heard Barb's voice, Jimmy turned and looked down at her for just a minute. Then he was gone, high up into the trees, home in the forest where he belonged.

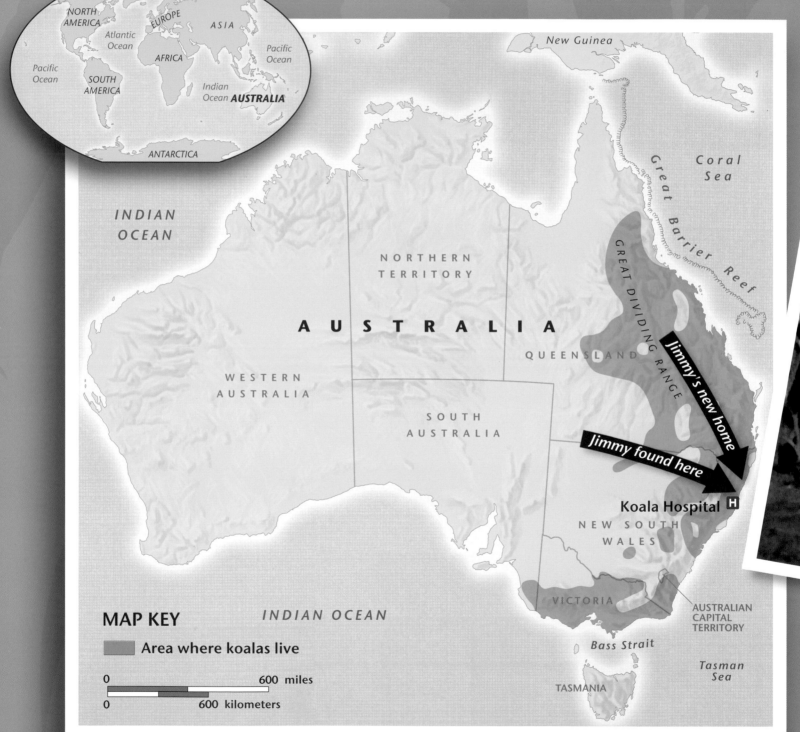

Jimmy's home and where koalas live

NORTH AMERICA

EUROPE

ASIA

Atlantic Ocean

AFRICA

Pacific Ocean

Pacific Ocean

SOUTH AMERICA

Indian Ocean **AUSTRALIA**

ANTARCTICA

New Guinea

Coral Sea

INDIAN OCEAN

NORTHERN TERRITORY

AUSTRALIA

GREAT BARRIER REEF

GREAT DIVIDING RANGE

QUEENSLAND

Jimmy's new home

WESTERN AUSTRALIA

SOUTH AUSTRALIA

Jimmy found here

Koala Hospital **H**

NEW SOUTH WALES

INDIAN OCEAN

VICTORIA

AUSTRALIAN CAPITAL TERRITORY

Bass Strait

TASMANIA

Tasman Sea

MAP KEY

Area where koalas live

0   600 miles

0   600 kilometers

All about Jimmy and koalas

- Koalas aren't bears, but rather a kind of mammal called a marsupial (like kangaroos, wombats, and opossums). A mother koala carries her baby in a pouch on her body. Her newborn joey is blind and has no fur.

- Australia is the only place on Earth where koalas live in the wild. They are mostly active at night, and they sleep 18 to 20 hours a day.

- Koalas get most of their food and water from the leaves, stems, flowers, and bark of eucalyptus (also called gum) trees. The word "koala" means "little drink" in an Australian Aboriginal language.

- Eucalyptus leaves naturally contain chemicals that are poisonous to most animals. Koalas can digest a certain amount of these toxic chemicals, and they sniff each leaf before chewing to make sure it's safe to eat.

- Susan Kelly has more than 1,000 hours of footage of Jimmy and other koalas at the Koala Hospital from the three years she spent filming them.

Note from the photographer

Susan Kelly says "hello" to Angus at the Koala Hospital.

Koalas are the real-life fairies of the forest. Big fluffy ears and bright shiny eyes look down at you from the tree canopy with a zen-like gaze and what appears to be a permanent half-smile on their face. One look into their eyes, and you're under their spell.

I came to work with koalas when I realized that despite being an Australian, a journalist, and an animal lover, I really knew nothing about them—except their reputation for sleeping most of the time.

To my surprise, when I began researching there was very little information available. When I asked others what they knew about koalas, it seemed few had ever seen one outside a zoo. I thought it was a shame that not much was widely known about Australia's adorable icon, so I set about telling their story through film over the next several years.

What I learned in the process was devastating. The cutting down of trees for new houses and roads is rapidly destroying koalas' wild habitat, and many that live near expanding suburbs are hurt and killed by dog attacks, car accidents, or stress-related disease. Koalas are now also listed as one of the top ten species most vulnerable to climate change. Higher temperatures from global warming have fueled massive forest fires and are increasing the levels of toxic chemicals in the eucalyptus leaves koalas must eat. All of these factors have had tragic consequences for koalas in the past decade.

Ultimately, this journey of discovery led me to the Port Macquarie Koala Hospital—the setting for my documentary—and Jimmy. This unique hospital has been caring for koalas for 40 years. For the most part, the koalas seem very accepting of the care they're given and appear genuinely pleased to see you when you walk into the room. They often will come over to say "hello"— koala style—by touching noses.

One of my most treasured moments is when Bev, a koala I'd been filming over two years of her life, reached out and held my hand in hers while she ate her leaves. It seemed like she was just happy to have me there with her.

It was truly a gift and brings tears to my eyes when I think about it, as sadly, Bev didn't make it out into the wild like our hero, Jimmy.

Through my work, I hope to share the delight I feel when I'm with koalas. To me, there is no greater joy than seeing a wild koala at home in the trees. I hope we will continue to see them living wild, high in the sky, looking down with that precious half-smile.

I'd like to pay tribute to all the kind folks at the Koala Hospital for their critically important work helping to save our furry global treasure. It's a special place with incredible people.

Deep gratitude also goes to my wondrous husband, family, and friends, who kindly support my koala addiction with love and generosity. I'm happy to say, they have all come to love koalas just as much as I do.

And last but never least, to you, dear reader, for your keen interest and for what you may do to help koalas survive into the future.

— Susan Kelly
Video journalist and filmmaker

Want to learn more about koalas?

WEBSITES

**animals.nationalgeographic.com/
animals/mammals/koala**
Fact page and range map of koalas
from National Geographic

**kids.nationalgeographic.com/kids/
animals/creaturefeature/koala**
Information and fast facts about
koalas from National Geographic Kids

www.koalahospital.com
Site for Susan Kelly's documentary
featuring Jimmy and the work to save
koalas at the Koala Hospital

www.koalahospital.org.au
Learn more about the Koala Hospital in Port Macquarie, Australia, and
adopt a koala

www.savethekoala.com
Site for the Australian Koala Foundation, a nonprofit organization dedicated to conserving koalas and
their habitat

BOOKS

Barwood, Lee. *Klassic Koalas: Ancient
Aboriginal Tales in New Retellings.*
Koala Jo Publishing, 2007.

Bishop, Nic. *Marsupials.* Scholastic
Inc., 2009.

Collard, Sneed. *Pocket Babies: And
Other Amazing Marsupials.* Lerner
Publishing Group, 2007.

Kalman, Bobbie, and Heather Levigne.
The Life Cycle of a Koala. Crabtree
Publishing Company, 2002.

Pohl, Kathleen. *Koalas/Koalas*
(English/Spanish). Gareth Stevens
Publishing, 2007.

Sharp, Ann. *The Koala Book.* Pelican
Publishing, 1995.

PLACES TO SEE KOALAS

In the United States
Cleveland Metroparks Zoo, 3900
Wildlife Way, Cleveland, Ohio

Los Angeles Zoo, 5333 Zoo Drive,
Los Angeles, California

Riverbanks Zoo and Garden, 500
Wildlife Parkway, Columbia,
South Carolina

San Diego Zoo, 2920 Zoo Drive,
San Diego, California

San Francisco Zoo, 1 Zoo Road,
San Francisco, California

Around the World
Cleland Conservation Park,
South Australia

Duisburg Zoo, Duisburg, Germany

Edinburgh Zoo, Scotland,
United Kingdom

Healesville Sanctuary, Victoria,
Australia

Koala Hospital, Port Macquarie,
Australia

Royal Melbourne Zoo, Victoria,
Australia

Schönbrunner Tiergarten, Vienna,
Austria

HELPING KOALAS

**You can help koalas like Jimmy the
joey no matter where you live in the
world.**

—Read about koalas, visit live koala
exhibits, and share what you learn
about koalas and the environmental
dangers they face

—Adopt a koala online from the
Koala Hospital

—Donate to the Koala Hospital or
other koala conservation groups

—Write to the Australian government
about protecting all koalas

In Australia, you can also:

—Contact the Koala Hospital if
you find a wounded, sick, or
stranded koala

—Help plant new eucalyptus trees,
where koalas can make their home

—Visit or volunteer at the Koala
Hospital, where Jimmy the joey
was rescued

In memory of Bev, Bea, and Sandy—three of my dearest koala friends,
who have now gone to the "great gum tree in the sky." —S. K.

For my high-climbing son, Ben, and to all the humans who work to
save and protect the koalas and their trees. —D. L. R.

Published by the National Geographic Society
John M. Fahey, *Chairman of the Board and Chief Executive Officer*
Timothy T. Kelly, *President*
Declan Moore, *Executive Vice President; President, Publishing and Digital Media*
Melina Gerosa Bellows, *Executive Vice President; Chief Creative Officer, Books, Kids, and Family*

Prepared by the Book Division
Hector Sierra, *Senior Vice President and General Manager*
Nancy Laties Feresten, *Senior Vice President, Kids Publishing and Media*
Jonathan Halling, *Design Director, Books and Children's Publishing*
Jay Sumner, *Director of Photography, Children's Publishing*

Jennifer Emmett, *Vice President, Editorial Director, Children's Books*
Eva Absher-Schantz, *Design Director, Kids Publishing and Media*
R. Gary Colbert, *Production Director*
Jennifer A. Thornton, *Director of Managing Editorial*

Staff for This Book
Kate Olesin, *Project Editor*
Kathryn Robbins, *Art Director*
Lori Epstein, *Senior Illustrations Editor*
Hillary Moloney, *Illustrations Editor*
Carl Mehler, *Director of Maps*
Grace Hill, Michael O'Connor, *Associate Managing Editors*
Joan Gossett, *Production Editor*
Ariane Szu-Tu, *Editorial Assistant*
Lewis R. Bassford, *Production Manager*
Susan Borke, *Legal and Business Affairs*

Manufacturing and Quality Management
Phillip L. Schlosser, *Senior Vice President*
Chris Brown, *Vice President, NG Book Manufacturing*
George Bounelis, *Vice President, Production Services*
Nicole Elliott, *Manager*
Rachel Faulise, *Manager*
Robert L. Barr, *Manager*

The font is set in Neutra Text.

In addition to the photographs by Susan Kelly, the book's images are credited as follows:
Cover: (log), Keattikorn/Shutterstock
Back Flap: (Susan Kelly), Tim Kelly; (Deborah Lee Rose), Ellen B. Smith
Eucalyptus used throughout design: Robyn Mackenzie/Shutterstock; Arkady/Shutterstock
p. 4, Daniel J. Cox/NaturalExposures.com; p. 6, Danita Delimont/Galo Images/Getty Images; p. 17, Gerry Walsh/Koala Hospital; map, National Geographic Maps

A note on the design: Certain types of eucalyptus trees have a rainbow of colors in their bark. The background colors in this book reflect that variety. The borders are traditional Australian Aboriginal designs based on a dot painting depicting a river.

CELEBRATING
◀ **125** ▶
YEARS

The National Geographic Society is one of the world's largest nonprofit scientific and educational organizations. Founded in 1888 to "increase and diffuse geographic knowledge," the Society's mission is to inspire people to care about the planet. It reaches more than 400 million people worldwide each month through its official journal, *National Geographic,* and other magazines; National Geographic Channel; television documentaries; music; radio; films; books; DVDs; maps; exhibitions; live events; school publishing programs; interactive media; and merchandise. National Geographic has funded more than 10,000 scientific research, conservation, and exploration projects and supports an education program promoting geographic literacy.

For more information, please visit www.nationalgeographic.com, call 1-800-NGS LINE (647-5463), or write to the following address:
National Geographic Society
1145 17th Street N.W.
Washington, D.C. 20036-4688 U.S.A.

Visit us online at nationalgeographic.com/books

For librarians and teachers:
ngchildrensbooks.org

More for kids from National Geographic:
kids.nationalgeographic.com

For information about special discounts for bulk purchases, please contact National Geographic Books Special Sales: ngspecsales@ngs.org

For rights or permissions inquiries, please contact National Geographic Books Subsidiary Rights: ngbookrights@ngs.org

Hardcover ISBN: 978-1-4263-1371-4
Library edition ISBN: 978-1-4263-1372-1

Printed in Hong Kong
14/THK/2